102 Ways to Profit
Making Mini Etching Presses

Ritchie's Perfect Press - Seattle

102 Ways to Profit Making Mini Etching Presses
By Bill H. Ritchie

© 2024 Bill H. Ritchie
Ritchie's Perfect Press
Division of Emeralda Works, LLC
500 Aloha Street Unit 105
Seattle WA 98109
ISBN 9798877215245

Contents

Added resource 113

Proof of sale on Etsy 114

Actual screenshot from Etsy on sale of one Mini Etching Press

Date	Type	Description	Amount	Fee and tax	Net	Balance
Dec 30, 2023	Sale	Payment for Order #3157994933	$1,715.58	--	$1,715.58	$1,715.58
Dec 30, 2023	Fee	Processing fee Order #3157994933 3.0% of the order total plus $0.25	--	-$51.72	-$51.72	$1,663.86
Dec 30, 2023	Tax	Sales tax paid by buyer Order #3157994933 Remitted to tax authorities	--	-$115.86	-$115.86	$1,548.00
Dec 30, 2023	Fee	Transaction fee: Mini Etching Press 6276 Order #3157994933 6.5% of item total	--	-$97.18	-$97.18	$1,450.82
Dec 30, 2023	Fee	Transaction fee: Shipping Order #3157994933 6.5% of shipping total	--	-$6.81	-$6.81	$1,444.01

Cost of goods	**– $ 875.00**
Gross net	**$ 569,01**
Shipping	**– $ 108.50**
Net profit	**$ 460.51**

About me 115

What's next? 118

Introduction: If you love printmaking...

People who make prints sometimes use presses, although not all printing methods need presses. There are, however, one-hundred-and-one reasons profits are made making mini etching presses for sale to printmakers, teachers, and institutions who would like them.

How did I come up with this idea? First, I lived it. Loving printmaking, I made prints for sixty years, loving printmaking all the way. Second, I taught it in college as if I loved teaching printmaking for twenty of those years. Third, zealously, I wanted to share printmaking with massive numbers of people, more people, than go to art school!

Fourth, I evangelized for printmaking, taking what I learned in college I took this message around the world: *Print is the ancestor of all technologies*. To understand the roots of technology, one needs to study new technologies like video and computer graphics.

So awesome was my mission that the college in those days could not support it, so I quit my job to take it on myself. But having sold my big, college-sized presses, I had a problem: *No press!*

Luckily, a steel wright and engineer, Tom, built me to presses. One was as big as my first but more beautiful, and a model one-fourth its size. Luckily, people liked the little one better! The rest is the history of the Mini Halfwood Press – now an encyclopedia online.

The first four steps took *two generations*! In another twenty years, my mission includes these lists – volume 1, why make minis and, 2, reasons to profit by making them available to a big market.

A friend remarked that in manufacturing, there is an order of magnitude from the manufacturing investment to the retail price. If a press costs X to make, it might sell for 10X. A hundred-dollar cost retails for a thousand dollars. Many factors make up the profit margin.

If you love printmaking like I do, consider the reasons for making mini presses I made, the book, "101 Reasons to make Mini Etching Presses." Here there was an overriding factor, which is new technologies, not talked about. AI is one that, without it, increased the reasons by an order of magnitude. I used this to explain my love of printmaking for the hundred benefits it provides everyone, from the maker to the user and everyone in the supply and support chain.

This book is that book's companion list but now the focus is on profits. I am a teaching artist, and the first time I saw an etching press was in 1961 when I was 20. It was small, probably no bigger than a 12-inch-wide bed. Now, late in life, I wish it had been a mini, like one of the presses I use today showing kids how to print. Its bed is 6 inches wide.

Because if, back in 1961, it had been a Mini Etching Press, I would have saved tens of thousands of dollars of my money and my students' money. Moreover, the place of printmaking would have been far more important than it is today.

Printmaking would be a contender for extending STEM to STREAM!

Back in the 20th Century it was not the fault of teachers. How could they have known what I know now? They were born too soon. Art schools taught that printmaking was an orphan of uncertain ancestry, fostered in the realms of painting, commercial publishing, entertainment and hobbies.

Nowhere was it taught as all-important art and technology, joined at birth. Not until I came along and refused to follow the canon.

It is up to me to teach this and rejoin art am technology, the "Siamese twins" that made the worlds' civilizations what they are today.

To learn how this happened, read my autobiography, Volumes 1 and 2, link to Volume 2 here:

Reasons to be an optimist

Along with these 101 reasons to profit I prompted ChatGPT to list ten general areas where positive developments in sustainability and environmental conservation occurred in the past decade. I relate making mini etching presses for the Printmaking Schoolbox to these responses to my prompt for reasons to be optimistic for kids by ChatGPT:

1. Renewable Energy Advancements: Increased adoption and technological advancements in renewable energy sources like solar, wind, and hydro power, contributing to a reduction in carbon emissions.

2. Global Conservation Initiatives: Collaborative efforts and international agreements aimed at preserving biodiversity and protecting ecosystems, leading to positive outcomes for various species and habitats.

3. Innovations in Carbon Capture: Breakthroughs in carbon capture and storage technologies, helping to mitigate the impact of greenhouse gas emissions from industrial processes and power generation.

4. Advancements in Sustainable Agriculture: Implementation of sustainable farming practices, precision agriculture, and the development of eco-friendly alternatives to traditional farming methods.

5. Ocean Conservation Efforts: Increased attention and measures to protect marine ecosystems, combat overfishing, and address plastic pollution in the oceans.

6. Afforestation and Reforestation Initiatives: Global efforts to plant trees and restore forests, contributing to carbon sequestration and biodiversity conservation.

7. Green Transportation Solutions: Expansion of electric vehicles, improvements in public transportation infrastructure, and the adoption of sustainable urban mobility practices.

8. Circular Economy Practices: Growing adoption of circular economy principles, promoting the reuse, recycling, and reduction of waste in various industries.

9. *Community-Led Environmental Initiatives: Grassroots movements and community-driven projects focusing on local environmental issues, fostering a sense of responsibility and sustainability.*

10. *Climate Resilience and Adaptation Measures: Implementation of strategies and policies to enhance communities' resilience to climate change, including infrastructure improvements and disaster preparedness.*

Some software like Generative Pre-trained Transformers (GPT) give me reasons to believe in both technology *and* human intelligence may help save Earth's human and other life sustainability. Now, AI might be added to our toolkit in curriculum design for a series of printmaking subscription boxes.

However, there are huge considerations and risks, the main being that AI may hurry mass extinction of humankind and all that I and other artists love about Nature along with it, a perfect storm of human stupidity and Natural responses to climate change, for example.

By reinventing printmaking in such ways and by such means as a Printmaking Schoolbox product line, beginning with the end in mind of helping very young learners with skills and knowledge about printmaking, such innate satisfaction for curiosity and anticipation may help build a framework for creative problem solving and lifelong learning.

1. Age and gender distribution

The combination of educational trends, a growing interest in hobbies, the rise of DIY culture, and a cultural shift towards handmade goods creates a lucrative market for hand printmaking tools and equipment, especially in the context of small, personal hand-operated presses. This industry can thrive by catering to diverse age groups, educational institutions, and the broader demand for unique, personalized, and hands-on creative experiences.

2. Rising Interest in DIY Projects

The growing trend of do-it-yourself (DIY) projects among various age groups, especially millennials and Gen Z, has created a demand for tools and equipment that facilitate creative expression. Hand printmaking aligns with this trend, making it a lucrative market.

3. Popularity in Homeschooling

With the rise in homeschooling, parents are seeking engaging and hands-on activities for their children. Hand printmaking tools offer an artistic outlet that not only supports education but also fosters creativity, making them attractive for homeschooling families.

4. Appeal to Diverse Age Groups

Printmaking appeals to individuals of all ages, from children to seniors. The versatility of hand-operated presses allows people of different ages to engage in this artistic activity, making the market broad and diverse.

5. Subscription Box Culture

The popularity of subscription boxes has grown significantly. Offering curated packages of printmaking tools and equipment on a subscription basis can tap into the market's desire for convenience and surprise, providing enthusiasts with new tools to experiment with regularly.

6. Rising Trend in Hobbies

Hobbies are becoming an integral part of people's lives, offering stress relief and a creative outlet. Hand printmaking tools cater to the growing interest in unique and personalized hobbies, driving demand for specialized equipment.

7. Art Programs in Schools and College

Many educational institutions are emphasizing art programs to foster creativity and critical thinking. Hand printmaking tools and equipment can become essential in these programs, creating a steady demand from educational institutions.

8. Social Exchange Among Printmakers

The community aspect of printmaking is significant. Social media platforms and local groups provide a space for printmakers to exchange ideas, techniques, and completed works. This sense of community can drive sales as enthusiasts seek to enhance their craft with new tools and equipment.

9. Personalization and Customization Trend

The modern consumer values personalized and unique items. Hand printmaking allows individuals to create one-of-a-kind pieces, contributing to the broader trend of customization in various consumer goods.

10. Therapeutic Benefits

Printmaking is often considered therapeutic, offering a meditative and stress-relieving activity. As awareness of mental health benefits continues to grow, hand printmaking tools become sought after for their ability to provide a creative and calming outlet.

11. Cultural Shift Towards Handcrafted Goods

There is a cultural shift towards appreciating handmade and artisanal products. Hand-operated presses fit into this narrative, contributing to the appeal of small-scale, personalized, and handcrafted art, making the market more lucrative.

12. Global distribution and new technology

The impact of globalization on the manufacturing of hand printmaking tools opens up numerous opportunities for profitability. Leveraging global technologies, accessing diverse markets, collaborating on research, and adapting products to international preferences are key factors that indicate a lucrative business environment for the research and development of hand-operated printing presses suitable for the 21st century.

13. Technological Advancements

Globalization has facilitated the exchange of technological innovations. Incorporating cutting-edge materials and manufacturing processes from around the world into hand printmaking tools enhances their performance, durability, and appeal, driving profitability through superior products.

14. Access to Global Markets

Manufacturers now have unprecedented access to global markets. By developing hand-operated printing presses with features catering to diverse artistic preferences worldwide, businesses can tap into a broader customer base, expanding sales and profitability.

15. Collaborative Research Opportunities

Globalization fosters collaboration between researchers and experts across borders. Engaging in international research partnerships allows businesses to stay at the forefront of printmaking technology, ensuring their products remain innovative and competitive.

16. Educational Integration on a Global Scale

With the globalization of education, hand printmaking tools designed for educational purposes can find a market worldwide. Adapting tools to meet the needs of different educational systems and curricula creates a significant avenue for profitability.

17. Cultural Adaptation and Customization

Globalization allows manufacturers to tailor hand printmaking tools to different cultural preferences. Customizing products based on regional artistic styles or preferences ensures that the tools resonate with a diverse global audience, driving increased sales.

18. Efficient Supply Chain Management

Globalization has led to improvements in supply chain management. Businesses can leverage these advancements to streamline production, reduce costs, and increase overall efficiency, contributing to higher profit margins in the manufacturing process.

19. Digital Integration for Educational Tools

The 21st century has seen a significant shift towards digital integration in education. Developing hand printmaking tools that can seamlessly integrate with digital platforms and resources enhances their educational value, making them more attractive in modern learning environments.

20. E-commerce Opportunities.

Globalization has fueled the growth of e-commerce. By establishing a strong online presence and leveraging international shipping networks, manufacturers can reach a global customer base, opening up new avenues for sales and revenue.

21. . Market Trends and Insights

Access to global markets provides valuable insights into emerging trends and preferences. Staying attuned to these trends enables manufacturers to adapt their product offerings, ensuring they remain relevant and in demand, ultimately contributing to sustained profitability.

22 International Investment Opportunities

Globalization creates opportunities for international investments. Manufacturers in the hand printmaking tools industry can attract investment from various sources globally, allowing for expanded research and development efforts, leading to more advanced and market-responsive products.

23. Resources and sustainability

The "small is beautiful" approach in the design and manufacturing of small, hand-operated printing presses offers numerous advantages in times of limited resources and shifting attitudes toward sustainability. By emphasizing resource efficiency, reduced environmental impact, localized production, and a focus on craftsmanship, companies can position themselves for long-term success in a market that values sustainability and innovation. Early investment in research and development aligned with these principles can ensure the survival and prosperity of businesses in the evolving landscape of the printing industry.

24. Resource Efficiency

Small, hand-operated printing presses typically require fewer raw materials compared to their larger counterparts. This resource efficiency makes them advantageous in times of limited resources, contributing to cost-effectiveness and sustainability in manufacturing.

25. Reduced Environmental Impact

Smaller components and designs often result in a reduced environmental footprint. Manufacturing processes that consume less energy and produce fewer emissions align with modern sustainability goals, making the product more appealing to environmentally conscious consumers.

26. Adaptability to Localized Production

Small-scale components enable localized production, reducing the need for extensive transportation of materials and finished products. This localized approach aligns with sustainable practices, as it minimizes the carbon footprint associated with the manufacturing process.

27. Skill Development in Local Communities

The manufacturing of small, hand-operated printing presses encourages skill development at the local level. Investing in human skills and knowledge fosters a sense of community empowerment and sustainability, as skilled workers become valuable assets to both the company and the community.

28. Promotion of Craftsmanship

Small-scale components often involve intricate craftsmanship. Promoting craftsmanship not only ensures the production of high-quality products but also fosters an appreciation for the artistry involved. This aligns with consumer preferences for unique, handcrafted items, contributing to sustained profitability.

29. Flexibility in Design Innovation

Small-scale components offer greater flexibility in design innovation. Manufacturers can adapt to changing market demands more quickly, introducing new features and improvements to stay ahead of the competition. This adaptability is crucial for long-term profitability in a rapidly evolving market.

30. Easier Recycling and Upcycling

Smaller components are generally easier to recycle or upcycle at the end of a product's life cycle. This aligns with the principles of a circular economy, where materials are reused or repurposed, contributing to a more sustainable and environmentally friendly manufacturing process.

31. Local Sourcing of Materials

Small-scale manufacturing allows for easier sourcing of materials locally. This reduces dependence on global supply chains, making the production process more resilient to disruptions and contributing to a sustainable business model that emphasizes local economic development.

32. Consumer Preference for Sustainable Products

Modern consumers increasingly prioritize sustainability when making purchasing decisions. Companies investing in the design and manufacturing of small, hand-operated printing presses with sustainability as a focus are likely to attract environmentally conscious consumers, driving sales and long-term profitability.

33. The purpose then and now

By addressing the needs of a broader population of influencers, including those promoting STEAM education and project-based learning, manufacturers can tap into a profitable market that values the flexible and artistic aspects of print in education. The market for small hand-operated printing presses is expanding because of their alignment with modern educational trends. Educators are seeking tools that are affordable, adaptable, safe, and conducive to fostering creativity and interdisciplinary learning.

34. Integration into STEAM Education

Small hand-operated printing presses align with the STEAM (Science, Technology, Engineering, Arts, and Mathematics) education framework. Educators are increasingly recognizing the value of incorporating art into STEM subjects, creating a demand for tools that can seamlessly integrate into diverse educational contexts.

35. Project-Based Learning Initiatives

The shift towards project-based learning emphasizes hands-on, experiential education. Small printing presses offer a practical and artistic dimension to projects, allowing students to explore and express their creativity in a tangible way, fostering a deeper understanding of the subject matter.

36. Affordability and Accessibility

Small presses are generally more affordable than large, traditional printing presses. This makes them accessible to a broader range of educational institutions, including those with limited budgets, providing opportunities for schools and community centers to incorporate printmaking into their programs.

37. Adaptability to Limited Space

Large presses require significant space, which can be a limitation for many educational institutions. Small presses are more adaptable to limited spaces, making them suitable for schools with smaller art studios or those aiming to integrate printmaking into existing or multipurpose classrooms and makerspaces.

38. Enhanced Safety Features

Small hand-operated printing presses often come with improved safety features. This makes them more suitable for educational settings, where the priority is to create a safe, appropriate, and inclusive learning environment for students of all ages.

39. Promotion of Artistic Exploration

Small presses encourage artistic exploration on an individual level. They provide a platform for students to experiment with printmaking techniques without the need for extensive resources, fostering a sense of creativity and artistic expression.

40. Facilitation of Interdisciplinary Learning

Small presses lend themselves well to interdisciplinary projects like STEM. Educators can integrate printmaking into various subjects, promoting cross-disciplinary learning experiences that resonate with modern educational philosophies.

41. Emphasis on Sustainable Practices

Designers of small presses are often aligned with sustainable practices, with awareness toward using fewer resources and producing less waste and recycling. Educators seeking to instill environmental consciousness in their students may be drawn to these smaller, more sustainable alternatives.

42. Engagement in Community Outreach

Small presses facilitate community outreach programs. Educational institutions can use these presses to engage with the local community, offering workshops and events that showcase the artistic and educational value of printmaking extensible to non-traditional living spaces.

43. Fostering a Culture of Inclusivity

The accessibility and affordability of small presses contribute to a culture of inclusivity in art education. They allow educational institutions to provide printmaking opportunities to a more diverse student population, ensuring that art is a medium accessible to all.

44. Education and entertainment trends

The integration of small, even toy-like printing presses into innovative educational and entertainment products offers a range of opportunities for companies to tap into a lucrative market. By combining play with learning, these products can provide enriching experiences that promote creativity, problem-solving skills, and a love for artistic expression from an early age.

45. Interactive Learning Games

Toy printing presses can be incorporated into interactive learning games that engage children in educational activities. These games can focus on teaching basic art concepts, colors, shapes, and even early printing techniques, turning the learning process into a playful and enjoyable experience.

46. Storytelling and Creativity Kits

Create storytelling and creativity kits that include toy printing presses. Children can use these kits to illustrate their own stories, fostering creativity, and enhancing literacy skills while introducing them to the world of printmaking in a fun and imaginative way.

47. STEM/STEAM Educational Toys

Develop STEM/STEAM educational toys that incorporate printing presses as part of a broader learning experience. Integrate elements of science, technology, engineering, and math (STEM), or include art to make it STEAM-focused, encouraging a holistic and multidisciplinary approach to education through play.

48. Customizable Craft Sets

Design toy printing presses as part of customizable craft sets. Children can personalize their printing projects, allowing for self-expression and creativity. This not only teaches artistic skills but also reinforces the idea that learning can be a personalized and enjoyable experience. It is another way to enter the growing market for art subscription boxes.

49. Educational Board Games

Integrate toy printing presses into educational board games that require problem-solving and strategic thinking. This approach combines entertainment with learning, making it an attractive option for parents and educators looking for engaging and enriching activities for children.

50. Augmented Reality (AR) Experiences

Explore augmented reality (AR) experiences that involve toy printing presses as well as professional, small, hand-operated presses. AR technology can enhance the learning process by providing additional information, animations, or interactive elements, making the play more immersive and educational.

51. Collaborative Learning Sets

Develop collaborative learning sets that include multiple toy printing presses. This encourages teamwork and social interaction among children as they work together on printing projects, promoting communication and cooperation skills. Combined with distance learning and home school this makes for a profitable business model.

52. Integration with Digital Platforms

Connect toy printing presses with digital platforms or apps that provide additional learning resources and activities. This blend of physical and digital learning creates a dynamic and interactive educational experience for children. The scalability of this approach makes the small printing press a profitable item.

53. Incorporation into DIY Science Kits

Integrate toy printing presses into do-it-yourself (DIY) science kits. This approach combines creativity with scientific exploration, allowing children to experiment with different printing materials and techniques while learning about the principles of art and science, technology, engineering, and even mathematics (STEAM).

54. Themed Learning Sets

Create themed learning sets that incorporate toy printing presses into specific educational themes. For example, a set centered around historical periods or famous artists can introduce children to art history while they enjoy hands-on printing activities. Integrating properties like "Rembrandt's Press," come to mind, making profitability even more likely.

55. STEM to STEAM

Small, hand-operated printing presses designed for early childhood education offer a holistic approach to learning, encompassing fine motor skills, cognitive development, emotional expression, and social interaction. By empowering educators with tools that enhance these essential aspects of early childhood education, manufacturers can tap into a market that values comprehensive and enriching learning experiences for young children, making their production both purposeful and profitable.

56. Early Introduction to Fine Motor Skills

Small, hand-operated printing presses designed for early childhood education can contribute to the development of fine motor skills in young children. Activities involving pressing, rolling, and manipulating printing tools enhance hand-eye coordination, dexterity, and precision, setting a foundation for future academic and practical skills.

57. Multisensory Learning Experiences

Printing engages multiple senses, including touch, sight, and sometimes even smell. Incorporating small printing presses into early childhood education provides multisensory learning experiences, which are known to enhance cognitive development and memory retention, making the educational process more effective and enjoyable.

58. Language and Vocabulary Development

Printmaking activities involve verbal communication and discussions about the creative process. Educators can use small printing presses to introduce and reinforce vocabulary related to colors, shapes, textures, and artistic concepts, fostering language development in young children.

59. Cognitive and Mathematical Concepts

Printing involves planning and sequencing steps, introducing basic cognitive and mathematical concepts. Educators can use small printing presses to teach children about patterns, counting, and spatial relationships, laying the groundwork for future understanding of more complex mathematical concepts.

60. Expressive Art and Emotional Development

Artistic expression through printing allows children to convey their emotions and thoughts. Integrating small printing presses into early childhood education supports expressive art, providing a medium for children to communicate and process their feelings, contributing to emotional development.

61. Storytelling and Literacy Integration

Printing can be integrated into storytelling activities, where children create their own illustrated stories. This not only promotes literacy but also enhances creativity and imagination, making the learning process more engaging for young learners.

62. Social and Collaborative Learning

Small printing presses encourage social interaction and collaboration among children. Group activities involving printing promote teamwork, sharing, and communication skills, fostering a sense of community and social development in early childhood education.

63. Introduction to Cultural and Historical Concepts

Printing has played a significant role in shaping cultures and histories. Educators can use small printing presses to introduce young children to cultural and historical concepts, exploring diverse artistic traditions and encouraging an appreciation for the rich tapestry of human creativity.

64. Environmental Awareness and Sustainability

Educators can use small printing presses to teach young children about sustainability and the environment. Emphasizing the use of eco-friendly materials and practices in printing activities instills a sense of responsibility and environmental awareness from an early age.

65. Parental Involvement and Home Extension Activities

Small printing presses can be incorporated into activities that involve parents or caregivers. Providing take-home printing projects encourages parental involvement in the child's education, creating a bridge between classroom learning and home experiences.

66. Aesthetics and beauty

The convergence of beauty, functionality, lower price, portability, and educational value in the design of small, hand-operated printing presses creates a compelling value proposition. Manufacturers that prioritize aesthetics alongside practicality can tap into a profitable market by appealing to a broader range of consumers, including artists, educators, and design enthusiasts who value the marriage of form and function in their creative tools and multidisciplinary studios and classrooms.

67. Broader Market Appeal

Incorporating beauty into the design of small, hand-operated printing presses expands their market appeal beyond traditional users. Aesthetic considerations attract a wider range of consumers, including artists, educators, and hobbyists who may prioritize both functionality and visual appeal when choosing their tools.

68. Enhanced User Experience

Beautifully designed printing presses contribute to a positive and enjoyable user experience. The combination of functionality and aesthetics makes the printing process more engaging, encouraging users to spend more time on creative activities, which can drive increased usage and loyalty to the brand.

69. Attractive Educational Tools

Educational value is often enhanced by the aesthetics of tools. Beautifully designed printing presses can captivate the attention of students, making the learning process more enjoyable and memorable. Educators are likely to choose tools that not only serve a functional purpose but also contribute to a visually stimulating and enriching educational environment.

70. Portability and Versatility

Designing printing presses with portability in mind enhances their practicality for a variety of settings. Artists and educators appreciate tools that are not only functional and beautiful but also versatile and easy to transport, making them suitable for use in various locations and educational settings.

71. Integration of Sustainable Materials

Aesthetic considerations often align with a commitment to sustainability. Manufacturers can use eco-friendly and aesthetically pleasing materials in the construction of printing presses, appealing to environmentally conscious consumers who value both form and function.

72. Customization Options

Allowing for customization in the design of printing presses, such as color options or artistic embellishments, provides consumers with a sense of personalization. The ability to choose a tool that aligns with individual tastes and preferences enhances the overall value proposition, making the product more attractive to potential buyers.

73. Crossover Appeal to Design Enthusiasts

Beautifully designed printing presses can appeal not only to printmakers but also to design enthusiasts who appreciate well-crafted and aesthetically pleasing objects. This crossover appeal expands the potential customer base and can attract those who may not be traditional users but are drawn to the artistic aspect of the tool.

74. Affordability and Mass Market Penetration

Lowering the price point of aesthetically pleasing printing presses can make them more accessible to a broader audience. Affordable yet beautiful tools can penetrate the mass market, reaching a larger, mixed demography base and driving higher sales volumes.

75. Promotion of Artistic Expression

Beautifully designed printing presses contribute to the overall artistic expression of the user. Artists often appreciate tools that align with their creative sensibilities, enhancing the overall artistic process and making the printing press an integral part of their artistic and cultural identity.

76. Social Media and Shareability

Aesthetically pleasing tools are more likely to be shared on social media platforms. Users may showcase their beautifully designed printing presses, leading to organic marketing and increased visibility. This social media presence can attract new customers, contributing to the profitability of the manufacturing endeavor.

77. Cross technologies

The profitability of manufacturing handcrafted plate-making tools and printing presses lies in the unique value proposition they offer: an integration of traditional craftsmanship with modern digital technologies. This approach taps into niche markets, meets the demand for artisanal products, and positions manufacturers at the forefront of innovation in both traditional and digital printmaking for home, studio, and school. (See also *Resources: AI blog* at the end)

78. Heritage and Craftsmanship Appeal

Handcrafted printing plate-making tools evoke a sense of heritage and craftsmanship, appealing to a market that values tradition and the handmade. This appeal can drive sales among enthusiasts who appreciate the artistry and skill involved in creating such tools.

79. Niche Market for Artistic Expression

Artistic printmaking processes using handmade tools cater to a niche market of artists and printmakers seeking unique and expressive methods. The personalized nature of handmade tools makes them attractive to individuals who prioritize artistic expression and creativity in their work.

80. Demand for Limited Edition and Artisanal Products

The market values limited edition and artisanal products. Handmade printing plate-making tools facilitate the creation of exclusive prints, appealing to collectors and individuals who seek unique, one-of-a-kind items. This exclusivity can drive higher prices and profit margins.

81. Integration of Traditional and Digital Technologies

Innovations in handcrafted plate-making tools can extend into the digital age. Manufacturers can design tools that seamlessly integrate with digital technologies, such as the Internet of Things (IoT) and Extended Reality (XR), providing a bridge between traditional printmaking and modern digital processes.

82. Cross-Technological Applications

Hand-operated printing presses designed for integration with digital technologies offer cross-technological applications. For example, combining traditional plate-making with IoT sensors can enable data-driven print customization, opening up new possibilities for personalized and interactive printed materials.

83. Educational Value in Cross-Technology Learning

Hand-operated printing presses that incorporate digital technologies can be valuable educational tools. They provide a platform for students to learn both traditional printmaking techniques and modern digital integration, fostering a well-rounded understanding of the evolution of print technologies.

84. Customization and Personalization

Handmade tools allow for a high degree of customization. Integrating digital technologies enables further personalization, allowing users to experiment with different designs, patterns, and effects. This customization aspect appeals to a market that values bespoke and tailored products.

85. Art and Technology Fusion

The fusion of art and technology creates a unique value proposition. Hand-operated printing presses that embrace both traditional craftsmanship and modern digital capabilities cater to individuals who appreciate the synergy between artistic expression and technological innovation.

86. Storytelling and Brand Differentiation

The handcrafted nature of the tools, coupled with digital integration, provides a compelling storytelling opportunity for manufacturers. Brands can differentiate themselves by emphasizing the journey of creating tools that honor tradition while embracing the possibilities of the digital age.

87. Innovation in Digital Printmaking

Small, hand-operated printing presses designed for integration with digital technologies contribute to the innovation in the digital printmaking space. This innovation attracts forward-thinking artists, educators, and professionals who seek tools that push the boundaries of what is possible in the realm of print.

88. Flipping the studio and project-based learning

The profitability of manufacturing small, personal-sized printing presses for educational integration lies in their ability to contribute to the social aspects of learning. These tools not only facilitate collaborative and cross-disciplinary learning but also create communities of educators and students who actively engage with the products. Manufacturers benefit from the positive impact of their tools on the learning experience, fostering brand loyalty and word-of-mouth marketing within educational, professional, and family circles.

89. Collaborative Learning Communities

Small, personal-sized printing presses contribute to the creation of collaborative learning communities. Teachers and students can engage in collaborative printmaking projects, fostering a sense of teamwork and shared accomplishment. The social aspect of creating together enhances the overall learning experience.

90. Community Building and Sharing

The use of small printing presses encourages community building within educational settings. Students can share their printmaking experiences, techniques, and finished prints, creating a culture of sharing and mutual support. Manufacturers benefit from this community-building aspect as it amplifies the visibility and positive reputation of their products.

91. Student Empowerment and Ownership

The social aspect of making and sharing prints empowers students to take ownership of their creative processes. As they share their work within the classroom or wider community, students experience a sense of pride and accomplishment, reinforcing the value of the printing press as a tool for self-expression.

92. Cross-Disciplinary Collaboration

Small printing presses facilitate cross-disciplinary collaboration. Students can integrate printmaking into various subjects within STEAM, allowing for a holistic and interconnected learning experience. Manufacturers benefit from this versatility as their products become essential tools in cross-disciplinary educational approaches.

93. Showcasing Student Work

Manufacturers can leverage the social aspect of making and sharing prints by providing platforms for showcasing student work. This not only promotes the creative achievements of students but also serves as a marketing tool for the printing presses, as educators and institutions share success stories.

94. Professional Development and Networking

Manufacturers can organize workshops and training sessions that encourage professional development among educators. The social interaction during these events provides an opportunity for networking and sharing best practices, positioning the manufacturer as a supportive partner in the educational community.

95. Online Communities and Social Media Engagement

The rise of online communities and social media platforms allows manufacturers to build a virtual space for educators and users of their printing presses. Engaging with these communities creates a dialogue around the tools, fosters a sense of belonging, and encourages the sharing of innovative ideas and practices.

96. Competition, profit, and loss

The makers of large-scale printing presses lost market share by neglecting the niche opened by early innovators who focused on small, beautiful, functional, and educational hand-operated printing presses. Ignoring shifts in educational trends, inflexibility in product design, overlooking personalization, lack of engagement with educational communities, ignoring the appeal of handcrafted goods, and failing to embrace digital integration all contributed to their decline in a market where innovative and versatile solutions were becoming increasingly valued. (See sample accounting from Etsy sale)

97. Failure to Recognize Shifting Educational Trends.

Makers of large-scale printing presses may have lost market share by failing to recognize the shifting trends in education. The emphasis on hands-on, project-based learning and the integration of arts into STEM education created a demand for smaller, versatile, and educational hand-operated printing presses. Ignoring this niche market meant missing out on a growing segment of educators and students seeking innovative tools.

98. Inflexibility in Product Design and Size.

Large-scale presses are often designed for industrial or commercial printing purposes, lacking the flexibility and adaptability required for educational and recreational settings. Manufacturers who ignored the demand for smaller, beautiful, and functional presses missed the opportunity to cater to users looking for tools that are not only practical but also aesthetically pleasing and user-friendly.

99. Overlooking the Value of Personalization.

The niche market for small, hand-operated printing presses thrived on the value of personalization and individual expression. Makers of large-scale presses might have overlooked the growing interest in bespoke and customizable tools, leading to a missed opportunity to provide products that cater to users' desire for a sense of ownership and pride in their creative processes.

100. Lack of Engagement with Educational Communities.

Manufacturers of large-scale presses may have missed the chance to engage with the educational communities actively adopting small presses. Building relationships with educators, participating in workshops, and understanding the specific needs of these users could have informed the design of products better suited for educational settings. Ignoring such engagement hindered their ability to tap into this niche market.

101. Ignoring the Shift Towards Handcrafted Goods

The market has seen a growing appreciation for handcrafted, artisanal products. Makers of large-scale presses may not have adapted to the trend favoring smaller, hand-operated presses that embrace craftsmanship and personal touch. Ignoring this cultural shift meant missing an opportunity to align with consumer preferences for unique and beautifully crafted tools.

Bonus, #102. Failure to Embrace Digital Integration.

Small presses, designed with versatility and educational content in mind, often embrace digital arts integration in STEM, incorporating modern technologies like IoT and XR. Manufacturers of large-scale presses may have ignored the potential of integrating educational, recreational, and professional content into their designs. This oversight will later be seen as having hindered their ability to offer tools that cater to the evolving needs of users in the digital age.

Added resource
A blogger's article on AR, IoT, and XR

An article pressreader.com/blog added AR, more things as IoT and XR
1. Better integration with physical collections
2. AR seamlessly integrates with collections in physical libraries.
3. Patrons can use AR applications to access supplementary information about books, artifacts or artworks while browsing the physical shelves.

2. Collaboration and social interaction

Libraries are also hubs of community engagement and learning.

AR encourages social interaction by allowing multiple users to experience digital content together while remaining in the same physical space.

4. Superior accessibility and inclusivity
5. AR experiences are accessible to a much wider audience, including individuals with disabilities, as they rely on real-world physical elements. Libraries can use AR to provide inclusive learning opportunities where everyone can participate.

4. Cost-efficient: Implementing AR can be more cost-effective than VR, as it often requires fewer specialized devices and can run on standard smartphones or tablets.

Libraries can offer AR experiences without substantial financial investments.

This aspect is a great leveler as even smaller and rural libraries can join the technological revolution AR promises.

Proof of sale on Etsy

As a case in point, the author attached this spreadsheet showing the anatomy of the sale of a small, beautiful, and functional press, one of his original Halfwood Press Line. We no longer wish to make only high-costing presses to the exclusion of low costing presses. Our goal is to provide for the market of low-cost presses integrated in Printmaking Schoolbox products for education and play. These school boxes are known as subscription boxes which are enjoying a growing demand.

However, the demographic indicates a market for high-profile, high costing presses which will call attention to the lower cost presses. The buyer in this example is a retired person who bought the press for his family, the members of which include his 99-year-old mother who carved the blocks he planned to print, and his daughter, who is a teacher who will use the press in her classes. This is an ongoing story currently, part of the author's research and development of his enterprise.

(Next page)

Actual screenshot from Etsy on sale of one Mini Etching Press

Date	Type	Description	Amount	Fee and tax	Net	Balance
Dec 30, 2023	Sale	Payment for Order #3157994933	$1,715.58	--	$1,715.58	$1,715.58
Dec 30, 2023	Fee	Processing fee Order #3157994933 3.0% of the order total plus $0.25	--	-$51.72	-$51.72	$1,663.86
Dec 30, 2023	Tax	Sales tax paid by buyer Order #3157994933 Remitted to tax authorities	--	-$115.86	-$115.86	$1,548.00
Dec 30, 2023	Fee	Transaction fee: Mini Etching Press 6276 Order #3157994933 6.5% of item total	--	-$97.18	-$97.18	$1,450.82
Dec 30, 2023	Fee	Transaction fee: Shipping Order #3157994933 6.5% of shipping total	--	-$6.81	-$6.81	$1,444.01

Cost of goods	− $ 875.00
Gross net	$ 569,01
Shipping	− $ 108.50
Net profit	$ 460.51

About me

Born and raised on farms in central Washington State, I knew machines, and I loved to tinker when I was a kid. The nearest college was CWU, and I majored in arts and crafts. It was there I made etchings, along with screen-print, woodcut, and photography. Fast forward to when I was 63, I designed an etching press that was almost as much a work of art as I crafted it to look beautiful, but also as functional as any press I used.

Then my machinist friend, Tom Kughler, volunteered to make a model of it. I was joking when I said to him, "I wish I had a model to put on my fireplace mantle!" The rest is our history in making Mini Etching Presses. This is in our book titled *The Halfwood Press Encyclopedia*, available on amazon.

My intention today in writing these "101..." books is to encourage individuals, groups, companies and institutions to make Mini Etching presses for three reasons: Education, education, and education. They will profit. I could add, "a passion for printmaking" among these, but this is a businessperson's book, and I hesitate to mention the fuzzy, ineffable aspects of etching as an art form.

On the other hand, it turns out there are more scientific, technological, engineering, and mathematics besides profitable business in list the profitable considerations of making mini etching presses for fun and profit when education is brought into the scope of reasons for making Minis.

To print with the first mini Halfwood press, I had to inch away from that press I started out with in college. I had to pay my way to the "bigger and better presses" I used as a professor and professional printmaker. Finally I was older and had more sense and I set aside the notion. In 2004 I adopted "Small is beautiful," and this marked a turning point in my life.

Bill Gates taught that it is good to have your own company so you can experiment and test ideas on yourself, so I formed a company, the Perfect Press, a division of our family's Emeralda Works, LLC. Thus, fast forward another ten years and I had at long last graduated from the farm machines of my boyhood and college years to 21st-Century machine *language* so I can share the experience. I am a university-level researcher and teacher, and I tested the idea of profitable art and technology on myself. However, as a researcher, immediate profits are not my main interest. But the preceding profit table proves it is profitable to make a Mini Etching Press.

Like Bill Gates, in the beginning I didn't have to think about profits. I married well and was hired, at 24, into a plum job at the University of Washington. As a professor in a major research university I could teach, research, practice, and perform various services, all paid for by the State. At the end of two decades, I could retire young to continue the development of what I learned in college, equipped with 350 thousand dollars' worth of intellectual capital Washington State had invested in me for higher education.

Profit motive is everyone's concern, even in a teacher with sinecure, because profit is an aspect of civilization, trading and doing commerce with other people near and far. In keeping with doing service without immediate, vast profits, I enlisted the AI Large Language Model, ChatGPT3 in writing first the *Reasons for Making* and this "for profit" book to augment the basics of my teaching, research, practice, and service philosophy I learned in and out of college.

To make this list fast I augmented my original ten with AI to flesh out each of them, the elaboration making them more understandable. Profits will be made by those who make Mini Etching presses for any combination of reasons. This list is key to my vision of the Printmaking Schoolbox R&D as it may be realized by a business.

What's next?

When the right-sized, right priced small and beautiful hand-operated press is developed, tested, and found to be perfect for the task, it will be part of the subscription Printmaking Schoolbox and PrintPals. My hope is, of course, that I will be part of the success story.